TO

FROM

DATE

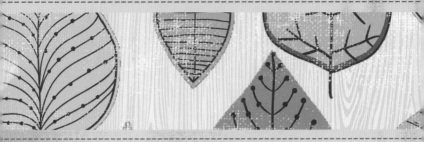

GOD IS IN CONTROL

Promises of Encouragement & Hope

Pi Pocket
INSPIRATIONS

Ellie Claire®
gift & paper expressions

...inspired by life

EllieClaire.com

Ellie Claire® Gift & Paper Expressions
Brentwood, TN 37027
EllieClaire.com

GOD IS IN CONTROL

Promises of Encouragement & Hope
A *Pocket Inspirations* Book

© 2014 by Ellie Claire
Ellie Claire is a registered trademark of Worthy Media, Inc.

ISBN 978-1-60936-954-5

Scripture references are from the following sources: The Holy Bible, King James Version (KJV).
The Holy Bible, New International Version®, NIV®. Copyright © 1973, 1978, 1984, 2011 by Biblica,
Inc.® All rights reserved worldwide. The Holy Bible, New King James Version® (NKJV). Copyright
© 1982 by Thomas Nelson, Inc. The Holy Bible, English Standard Version® (ESV), copyright © 2001
by Crossway Bibles, a publishing ministry of Good News Publishers. The New American Standard
Bible® (NASB), Copyright © 1960, 1962, 1963, 1968, 1971, 1972, 1973, 1975, 1977, 1995 by The
Lockman Foundation. The New Revised Standard Version Bible (NRSV). Copyright 1989, 1995,
Division of Christian Education of the National Council of the Churches of Christ in the United
States of America. The Holy Bible, New Living Translation (NLT), copyright 1996, 2004, 2007 by
Tyndale House Foundation. Used by permission of Tyndale House Publishers, Inc., Carol Stream,
Illinois 60188. *The Message* (MSG). Copyright © 1993, 1994, 1995, 1996, 2000, 2001, 2002. Used by
permission of NavPress Publishing Group. Used by permission. All rights reserved.

Excluding Scripture verses and deity pronouns, in some quotations references to men and masculine
pronouns have been replaced with gender-neutral or feminine references. Additionally, in some
quotations we have carefully updated verb forms and wording that may distract modern readers.

Stock or custom editions of Ellie Claire titles may be purchased in bulk for educational, business,
ministry, fundraising, or sales promotional use. For information, please e-mail info@EllieClaire.com.

Compiled by Joanie Garborg & Barbara Farmer
Designed by Gearbox | studiogearbox.com

Printed in China

CONTENTS

God [is] in control of our lives; nothing lies outside the realm of His redemptive grace.

— PENELOPE J. STOKES —

Introduction

Whatever the circumstances—sunshine or storm
clouds, serenity or chaos—our heavenly Father has
a plan. Nothing is an accident. We are not
left to chance. No twist of fate can surprise God,
for He is in control. And He is a God of promise:
He will always care for us, love us, guide us,
and He will never leave us alone.

God Is in Contol is a collection of Scripture, words
from God that He wants you to know. Quotations
filled with encouragement, grace, and love
complement each themed message. Let the sacred
passages and uplifting quotations meet you right
where you are, touching your heart and soul.

May you rest in God's promises and
live confidently in His providence—
in His mighty hand of protection and care—
both now and always.

God Is Our Refuge

God is our refuge and strength,
an ever-present help in trouble.
Therefore we will not fear,
though the earth give way
and the mountains fall into the heart of the sea,
though its waters roar and foam
and the mountains quake with their surging....
The Lord Almighty is with us;
the God of Jacob is our fortress.

PSALM 46:1-3, 7 NIV

You are my hiding place;
You preserve me from trouble;
You surround me with songs of deliverance.

PSALM 32:7 NASB

Hear my cry, O God;
Give heed to my prayer.
From the end of the earth I call to You
when my heart is faint;
Lead me to the rock that is higher than I.
For You have been a refuge for me,
A tower of strength against the enemy.
Let me dwell in Your tent forever;
Let me take refuge in the shelter of Your wings.

PSALM 61:1-4 NASB

When God has become...our refuge and our fortress, then we can reach out to Him in the midst of a broken world and feel at home while still on the way.

HENRI J. M. NOUWEN

The King of Kings

For God is the King of all the earth....
God reigns over the nations;
God sits on His holy throne.

PSALM 47:7-8 NKJV

Yours, O Lord, is the greatness and the power and
the glory and the victory and the majesty,
for all that is in the heavens and in the earth is
yours. Yours is the kingdom, O Lord, and you are
exalted as head above all. Both riches and honor
come from you, and you rule over all.
In your hand are power and might, and in your
hand it is to make great and to give strength
to all. And now we thank you, our God,
and praise your glorious name.

1 CHRONICLES 29:11-13 ESV

Ah Lord God! behold,
thou hast made the heaven and the earth
by thy great power and stretched out arm,
and there is nothing too hard for thee.

JEREMIAH 32:17 KJV

*God is not too great to be
concerned about our smallest wishes.
He is not only King and Ruler
of the universe, but also our
Father in Christ Jesus.*

BASILEA SCHLINK

Compassionate and Gracious

He made known his ways to Moses,
his acts to the people of Israel.
The LORD is merciful and gracious,
slow to anger and abounding in steadfast love.

PSALM 103:7-8 NRSV

Yet the LORD longs to be gracious to you;
therefore he will rise up to show you compassion.
For the LORD is a God of justice.
Blessed are all who wait for him!

ISAIAH 30:18 NIV

LORD, be gracious to us;
we long for you.
Be our strength every morning.

ISAIAH 33:2 NIV

The LORD bless you, and keep you;
The LORD make His face shine on you,
And be gracious to you;
The LORD lift up His countenance on you,
And give you peace.

NUMBERS 6:24-26 NASB

*Lord...give me only Your love
and Your grace.
With this I am rich enough,
and I have no more to ask.*

IGNATIUS OF LOYOLA

Awesome God

I will exalt you, my God the King;
I will praise your name for ever and ever.
Every day I will praise you
and extol your name for ever and ever.
Great is the LORD and most worthy of praise;
his greatness no one can fathom.
One generation commends your works to another;
they tell of your mighty acts.
They speak of the glorious splendor of your majesty—
and I will meditate on your wonderful works.
They tell of the power of your awesome works—
and I will proclaim your great deeds.
They celebrate your abundant goodness
and joyfully sing of your righteousness....
The Lord is righteous in all his ways,
and faithful in all he does.

PSALM 145:1-7, 17 NIV

The LORD is my strength and my song,
and he has become my salvation;
this is my God, and I will praise him....
Who is like you, O LORD, among the gods?
Who is like you, majestic in holiness,
awesome in glorious deeds, doing wonders?

EXODUS 15:2, 11 ESV

God's quest to be glorified and
our quest to be satisfied reach
their goal in this one experience:
our delight in God which
overflows in praise.

JOHN PIPER

His Renewing Word

You're my place of quiet retreat;

I wait for your Word to renew me....

Therefore I lovingly embrace everything you say.

PSALM 119:114, 119 MSG

You have dealt well with Your servant,

O LORD, according to Your word.

Teach me good discernment and knowledge,

For I believe in Your commandments.

Before I was afflicted I went astray,

But now I keep Your word.

You are good and do good;

Teach me Your statutes.

PSALM 119:65-68 NASB

Not one word has failed of all His good promise.

1 KINGS 8:56 NASB

All your words are true;
all your righteous laws are eternal.

PSALM 119:160 NIV

For the word of the Lord is right and true;
he is faithful in all he does.
The Lord loves righteousness and justice;
the earth is full of his unfailing love.

PSALM 33:4-5 NIV

*Be still, and in the quiet moments,
listen to the voice of your
heavenly Father. His words can
renew your spirit...no one knows you
and your needs like He does.*

JANET L. SMITH

Seeing the Unseen

Now faith is confidence in what we hope for
and assurance about what we do not see....
By faith we understand that the universe was formed
at God's command, so that what is seen
was not made out of what was visible....
And without faith it is impossible to please God,
because anyone who comes to him must
believe that he exists and that he
rewards those who earnestly seek him.

HEBREWS 11:1, 3, 6 NIV

We look not at the things which are seen,
but at the things which are not seen;
for the things which are seen are temporal,
but the things which are not seen are eternal.

2 CORINTHIANS 4:18 NASB

By faith Moses...regarded disgrace
for the sake of Christ as of greater value
than the treasures of Egypt, because he was
looking ahead to his reward.... He persevered
because he saw him who is invisible.

HEBREWS 11:24, 26-27 NIV

*Faith, as the Bible defines it,
is present-tense action.... It means
knowing something is real, this moment,
all around you, even when you dont
see it.... It's simply taking God at His
word and taking the next step.*

JONI EARECKSON TADA

Bless the Lord

Bless the Lord, O my soul,
and all that is within me,
bless his holy name!
Bless the Lord, O my soul,
and forget not all his benefits,
who forgives all your iniquity,
who heals all your diseases,
who redeems your life from the pit,
who crowns you with steadfast love and mercy,
who satisfies you with good
so that your youth is renewed like the eagle's.

PSALM 103:1-5 ESV

Bless the Lord, all you works of His,
in all places of His dominion.
Bless the Lord, O my soul!

PSALM 103:22 NASB

I will remember the deeds of the Lord;
yes, I will remember your wonders of old.
I will ponder all your work,
and meditate on your mighty deeds.
Your way, O God, is holy.
What god is great like our God?
You are the God who works wonders;
you have made known your might among the peoples.

PSALM 77:11–14 ESV

We worship You, we confess to You,
we praise You, we bless You,
we sing to You, and we give thanks
to You: Maker, Nourisher,
Guardian, Healer, Lord,
and Father of all.

LANCELOT ANDREWES

To Be Near God

Yet I am always with you;

you hold me by my right hand.

You guide me with your counsel,

and afterward you will take me into glory.

Whom have I in heaven but you?

And earth has nothing I desire besides you.

My flesh and my heart may fail,

but God is the strength of my heart

and my portion forever....

As for me, it is good to be near God.

I have made the Sovereign Lord my refuge.

PSALM 73:23-26, 28 NIV

God himself shall be with them, and be their God.

REVELATION 21:3 KJV

But let all who take refuge in you be glad;
let them ever sing for joy.
Spread your protection over them,
that those who love your name may rejoice in you.
For surely, LORD, you bless the righteous;
you surround them with your favor as with a shield.

PSALM 5:11-12 NIV

When I walk by the wayside,
He is along with me....
Amid all my forgetfulness of Him,
He never forgets me.

THOMAS CHALMERS

17

Above the Heavens

Lᴏʀᴅ, our Lord,

how majestic is your name in all the earth!

You have set your glory in the heavens....

When I consider your heavens,

the work of your fingers,

the moon and the stars,

which you have set in place,

what is mankind that you are mindful of them,

human beings that you care for them?

You have made them a little lower than the angels

and crowned them with glory and honor.

You made them rulers

over the works of your hands....

Lᴏʀᴅ, our Lord,

how majestic is your name in all the earth!

PSALM 8:1, 3-6, 9 NIV

Search high and low, scan skies and land,
you'll find nothing and no one quite like GOD.
The holy angels are in awe before him;
he looms immense and august
over everyone around him.
GOD-of-the-Angel-Armies, who is like you,
powerful and faithful from every angle?

PSALM 89:6-8 MSG

*Angels bright, heavens high,
waters deep, give God the praise.*

CHRISTOPHER COLLINS

More Precious
than Gold

The law of the Lord is perfect,
refreshing the soul.
The statutes of the Lord are trustworthy,
making wise the simple.
The precepts of the Lord are right,
giving joy to the heart.
The commands of the Lord are radiant,
giving light to the eyes.
The fear of the Lord is pure,
enduring forever.
The decrees of the Lord are firm,
and all of them are righteous.
They are more precious than gold,
than much pure gold.

PSALM 19:7-10 NIV

Listen as Wisdom calls out!...
"My words are plain to anyone with understanding,
clear to those with knowledge.
Choose my instruction rather than silver,
and knowledge rather than pure gold.
For wisdom is far more valuable than rubies.
Nothing you desire can compare with it."

PROVERBS 8:1, 9-11 NLT

God's work of giving wisdom is a means
to His chosen end of restoring and
perfecting the relationship between
Himself and human beings—the
relationship for which He made them.

J. I. PACKER

Forever and Ever

From you comes the theme of my praise....
The poor will eat and be satisfied;
those who seek the Lord will praise him—
may your hearts live forever!
All the ends of the earth
will remember and turn to the Lord,
and all the families of the nations
will bow down before him,
for dominion belongs to the Lord
and he rules over the nations.

PSALM 22:25-28 NIV

Grace and peace to you from him who is,
and who was, and who is to come.... To him be glory
and power for ever and ever! Amen.

REVELATION 1:4, 6 NIV

He is the living God and he endures forever;
his kingdom will not be destroyed,
his dominion will never end.

DANIEL 6:26 NIV

*Today Jesus is working just as
wonderful works as when He
created the heaven and the earth.
His wondrous grace, His
wonderful omnipotence,
is for His child who needs Him
and who trusts Him, even today.*

HURLBURT AND HORTON

The Path of Truth

I go to prepare a place for you.
And if I go and prepare a place for you,
I will come again and receive you to Myself;
that where I am, there you may be also.
And where I go you know, and the way you know.... I
am the way, the truth, and the life.
No one comes to the Father except through Me.

JOHN 14:2-4, 6 NKJV

Search me, O God, and know my heart;
test me and know my anxious thoughts.
Point out anything in me that offends you,
and lead me along the path of everlasting life.

PSALM 139:23-24 NLT

How blessed all those in whom you live, whose lives
become roads you travel; they wind through lonesome
valleys, come upon brooks,
discover cool springs and pools brimming with rain!
God-traveled, these roads curve up the mountain, and at
the last turn—Zion! God in full view!

PSALM 84:5-7 MSG

Heaven often seems distant
and unknown, but if He who made
the road...is our guide,
we need not fear to lose the way.

HENRY VAN DYKE

Hear My Prayer

Our Father which art in heaven,
Hallowed be thy name.
Thy kingdom come.
Thy will be done in earth, as it is in heaven.
Give us this day our daily bread.
And forgive us our debts,
as we forgive our debtors.
And lead us not into temptation,
but deliver us from evil:
For thine is the kingdom,
and the power, and the glory, for ever.
Amen.

MATTHEW 6:9-13 KJV

Evening, and morning, and at noon, will I pray,
and cry aloud: and he shall hear my voice.

PSALM 55:17 KJV

I love the Lord because he hears my voice
and my prayer for mercy.
Because he bends down to listen,
I will pray as long as I have breath!

PSALM 116:1-2 NLT

I call on you, my God, for you will answer me;
turn your ear to me and hear my prayer.

PSALM 17:6 NIV

God listens in compassion and love,
just like we do when our children
come to us. He delights in our presence.

RICHARD J. FOSTER

Plans for Hope

How blessed is God!... Long before he laid
down earth's foundations, he had us in mind,
had settled on us as the focus of his love, to
be made whole and holy by his love. Long,
long ago he decided to adopt us into his
family through Jesus Christ. (What pleasure
he took in planning this!) He wanted us to
enter into the celebration of his lavish
gift-giving by the hand of his beloved Son.
It's in Christ that you, once you heard the
truth and believed it (this Message of your
salvation), found yourselves home free....
This signet from God is the first installment
on what's coming, a reminder that we'll get
everything God has planned for us, a praising
and glorious life.

EPHESIANS 1:3-6, 13-14 MSG

28

"For I know the plans I have for you," declares the LORD, "plans to prosper you and not to harm you, plans to give you hope and a future."

JEREMIAH 29:11 NIV

This is the real gift: you have been given the breath of life, designed with a unique, one-of-a-kind soul that exists forever. Priceless in value, you are handcrafted by God, who has a personal design and plan for you.

Like a Shepherd

He tends his flock like a shepherd:
He gathers the lambs in his arms
and carry them close to his heart.

ISAIAH 40:11 NIV

*Genuine love sees faces,
not a mass: the Good Shepherd
calls His own sheep by name.*

GEORGE A. BUTTRICK

The LORD is my shepherd;

I shall not want.

He makes me to lie down in green pastures;

He leads me beside the still waters.

He restores my soul;

He leads me in the paths of righteousness

For His name's sake.

Yea, though I walk through the valley

of the shadow of death,

I will fear no evil;

For You are with me;

Your rod and Your staff,

they comfort me.

You prepare a table before me

in the presence of my enemies;

You anoint my head with oil;

My cup runs over.

Surely goodness and mercy shall follow me

All the days of my life;

And I will dwell in the house of the LORD

Forever.

PSALM 23:1-6 NKJV

His Ways

O the depth of the riches both of
the wisdom and knowledge of God!
how unsearchable are his judgments,
and his ways past finding out!
For who hath known the mind of the Lord?
or who hath been his counsellor?

ROMANS 11:33-34 KJV

For my thoughts are not your thoughts,
neither are your ways my ways, declares the Lord.
For as the heavens are higher than the earth,
so are my ways higher than your ways,
and my thoughts than your thoughts.

ISAIAH 55:8-9 ESV

He is the Rock, his works are perfect,
and all his ways are just. A faithful God
who does no wrong, upright and just is he.

DEUTERONOMY 32:4 NIV

Teach me your ways so I may know you
and continue to find favor with you.

EXODUS 33:13 NIV

*In both simple and eloquent ways,
our infinite God personally reveals
glimpses of Himself in the finite.*

In God's Peace

He said, Go forth, and stand upon the mount before
the Lord. And, behold, the LORD passed by,
and a great and strong wind rent the mountains...but
the LORD was not in the wind: and after
the wind an earthquake; but the LORD was not in the
earthquake: and after the earthquake a fire;
but the LORD was not in the fire:
and after the fire a still small voice.

1 KINGS 19:11-12 KJV

I will make a covenant of peace with them;
it will be an everlasting covenant....
I will put my sanctuary among them forever.
My dwelling place will be with them;
I will be their God, and they will be my people.

EZEKIEL 37:26-27 NIV

The LORD is in His holy temple.
Let all the earth be silent before Him.

HABAKKUK 2:20 NASB

Be still, and know that I am God.

PSALM 46:10 NIV

*Drop Thy still dews of quietness
till all our strivings cease;
take from our souls the strain
and stress, and let our ordered lives
confess the beauty of Thy peace.*

JOHN GREENLEAF WHITTIER

His Powerful Word

For the word of God is living and active and sharper
than any two-edged sword,
and piercing as far as the division of soul and spirit,
of both joints and marrow, and able to judge
the thoughts and intentions of the heart.
And there is no creature hidden from His sight,
but all things are open and laid bare
to the eyes of Him with whom we have to do.

HEBREWS 4:12-13 NASB

With my whole heart I have sought You;
Oh, let me not wander from Your commandments!
Your word I have hidden in my heart,
That I might not sin against You....
I will delight myself in Your statutes;
I will not forget Your word.

PSALM 119:10-11, 16 NKJV

All Scripture is inspired by God and is useful
to teach us what is true and to make us realize
what is wrong in our lives. It corrects us when
we are wrong and teaches us to do what is right.

2 TIMOTHY 3:16 NLT

The Son is the radiance of God's glory
and the exact representation of his being,
sustaining all things by his powerful word.

HEBREWS 1:3 NIV

*When we give the Word of God
space to live in our heart,
the Spirit of God will use it to take root,
penetrating the earthiest recesses of our lives.*

KEN GIRE

No Worries

Can all your worries add a single moment
to your life?... Look at the lilies and how they
grow. They don't work or make their clothing,
yet Solomon in all his glory was not dressed
as beautifully as they are. And if God cares so
wonderfully for flowers that are here today and
thrown into the fire tomorrow, he will certainly
care for you. Why do you have so little faith?

And don't be concerned about what to eat and
what to drink. Don't worry about such things.
These things dominate the thoughts
of unbelievers all over the world,
but your Father already knows your needs.
Seek the Kingdom of God above all else,
and he will give you everything you need.

LUKE 12:25, 27-31 NLT

Do not fear, for I am with you; Do not anxiously
look about you, for I am your God. I will
strengthen you, surely I will help you, Surely I will
uphold you with My righteous right hand.

ISAIAH 41:10 NASB

Give all your worries and cares to God,
for he cares about you.

1 PETER 5:7 NLT

*Leave for a season the remembrance
of your troubles and dwell on the
lovingkindness of God, that you may
recover by gazing on Him.*

The Earth Is the Lord's

The earth is the LORD's, and the fulness thereof;
the world, and they that dwell therein.
For he hath founded it upon the seas,
and established it upon the floods.

PSALM 24:1-2 KJV

Holy, holy, holy is the LORD of hosts;
the whole earth is full of his glory!

ISAIAH 6:3 ESV

The voice of the LORD echoes above the sea.
The God of glory thunders.
The LORD thunders over the mighty sea....
The LORD rules over the floodwaters.
The LORD reigns as king forever.

PSALM 29:3, 10 NLT

The Lord is a great God
And a great King above all gods,
In whose hand are the depths of the earth,
The peaks of the mountains are His also.
The sea is His, for it was He who made it,
And His hands formed the dry land.

*Forbid that I should walk through
Your beautiful world with unseeing
eyes.... Forbid that under the low roof
of workshop or office or study
I should ever forget Your great
overarching sky.*

JOHN BAILLIE

Seek First His Kingdom

Look at the birds of the air, that they do not sow,
nor reap nor gather into barns, and yet your heavenly Father
feeds them. Are you not worth much more than they?
And who of you by being worried can add a single hour to his life?
And why are you worried about clothing?

Observe how the lilies of the field grow; they do not toil nor do
they spin, yet I say to you that not even Solomon in all his glory
clothed himself like one of these. But if God so clothes the grass
of the field, which is alive today and tomorrow is thrown into the
furnace, will He not much more clothe you? You of little faith!
Do not worry then, saying, "What will we eat?" or
"What will we drink?" or "What will we wear for clothing?"
For...your heavenly Father knows that you need
all these things. But seek first His kingdom and His righteousness,
and all these things will be added to you.

MATTHEW 6:26-33 NASB

In extravagance of soul
we seek His face.
In generosity of heart,
we glean His gentle touch.
In excessiveness of spirit,
we love Him and
His love comes back
to us a hundredfold.

TRICIA MCCARY RHODES

To All Generations

Lord, you have been our dwelling place in all
generations. Before the mountains were brought
forth, or ever you had formed the earth and the world,
from everlasting to everlasting you are God.

PSALM 90:1-2 ESV

Know therefore that the Lord your God is God;
he is the faithful God, keeping his covenant
of love to a thousand generations of those who love
him and keep his commands.

DEUTERONOMY 7:9 NIV

Your kingdom is an everlasting kingdom,
And Your dominion endures throughout
all generations.

PSALM 145:13 NKJV

From everlasting to everlasting the Lord's
love is with those who fear him, and his
righteousness with their children's children.

PSALM 103:17 NIV

I will sing of the mercies of the Lord for ever:
with my mouth will I make known thy faithfulness
to all generations.

PSALM 89:1 KJV

Generation after generation of Bible
readers find that in these pages we become
insiders to a conversation in which God
uses words to form and bless us, to teach
and guide us, to forgive and save us.

EUGENE PETERSON

Our Everlasting Light

Your love, O LORD,
reaches to the heavens,
your faithfulness to the skies.
Your righteousness
is like the mighty mountains,
your justice like the great deep....
How priceless is your unfailing love!
People find refuge
in the shadow of your wings.
They feast on the abundance of your house;
you give them drink from
your river of delights.
For with you is the fountain of life;
in your light we see light.

PSALM 36:5-9 NIV

The sun shall be no more your light by day,
nor for brightness shall the moon give you light;
but the LORD will be your everlasting light,
and your God will be your glory. Your sun shall
no more go down, nor your moon withdraw itself;
for the LORD will be your everlasting light.

ISAIAH 60:19-20 ESV

It is only when Christ dwells within
our hearts, radiating the pure light
of His love through our humanity,
that we discover who we are and what
we were intended to be.

WENDY MOORE

That I May Know Him

I ask...the God of our Master, Jesus Christ,
the God of glory—to make you intelligent and
discerning in knowing him personally, your eyes
focused and clear, so that you can see exactly what it
is he is calling you to do, grasp the immensity
of this glorious way of life he has for his followers,
oh, the utter extravagance of his work in us who trust
him—endless energy, boundless strength!

EPHESIANS 1:17-19 MSG

Thanks be to God, who in Christ always leads
us in triumphal procession, and through
us spreads the fragrance of the knowledge
of him everywhere. For we are the aroma
of Christ to God among those who are being
saved and among those who are perishing.

2 CORINTHIANS 2:14-15 ESV

I count all things to be loss in view of the surpassing value of knowing Christ Jesus my Lord.... That I may know Him and the power of His resurrection and the fellowship of His sufferings.

PHILIPPIANS 3:8, 10 NASB

What matters supremely is not the fact that I know God, but the larger fact which underlies it—the fact that He knows me. I am graven on the palms of His hands.

J. I. PACKER

My Joy and Delight

Trust in the Lord and do good;
Dwell in the land and cultivate faithfulness.
Delight yourself in the Lord;
And He will give you the desires of your heart.
Commit your way to the Lord,
Trust also in Him, and He will do it.
He will bring forth your righteousness as the light
And your judgment as the noonday...
The humble will inherit the land
And will delight themselves in abundant prosperity.

PSALM 37:1-6, 11 NASB

I delight to do thy will, O my God.

PSALM 40:8 KJV

Send out your light and your truth....
Let them lead me to your holy mountain,
to the place where you live.
There I will go to the altar of God,
to God—the source of all my joy.
I will praise you with my harp,
O God, my God!

PSALM 43:3-4 NLT

Our fulfillment comes in knowing
God's glory, loving Him for it,
and delighting in Him. Our joy comes
from knowing He delights in us.

Perfect Peace

Don't worry about anything; instead,
pray about everything. Tell God what you need,
and thank him for all he has done.
Then you will experience God's peace,
which exceeds anything we can understand.
His peace will guard your hearts and minds
as you live in Christ Jesus.

PHILIPPIANS 4:6-7 NLT

You will keep in perfect peace
those whose minds are steadfast,
because they trust in you.
Trust in the LORD forever,
for the LORD, the LORD,
is the Rock eternal.

ISAIAH 26:3-4 NIV

Therefore, having been justified by faith, we have peace with God through our Lord Jesus Christ.

ROMANS 5:1 NASB

The Lord will give strength to His people;
The Lord will bless His people with peace.

PSALM 29:11 NKJV

Peace I leave with you; my peace I give to you. Not as the world gives do I give to you. Let not your hearts be troubled, neither let them be afraid.

JOHN 14:27 ESV

The God of peace gives perfect peace to those whose hearts are stayed upon Him.

CHARLES H. SPURGEON

God Revealed

The basic reality of God is plain enough.
Open your eyes and there it is! By taking a long
and thoughtful look at what God has created,
people have always been able to see what their eyes
as such can't see: eternal power, for instance,
and the mystery of his divine being.

ROMANS 1:19-20 MSG

Blessed be the name of God from age to age,
for wisdom and power are his. He changes times and
seasons, deposes kings and sets up kings;
he gives wisdom to the wise and knowledge
to those who have understanding. He reveals deep
and hidden things; he knows what
is in the darkness, and light dwells with him.

DANIEL 2:20-22 NRSV

The secret things belong to the LORD our God,
but the things revealed belong to us
and to our children forever, that we may follow
all the words of this law.

DEUTERONOMY 29:29 NIV

*The Lord's chief desire is to reveal
Himself to you.... He touches you,
and His touch is so delightful that,
more than ever,
you are drawn inwardly to Him.*

JEANNE GUYON

A New Power

A new power is in operation. The Spirit of life
in Christ, like a strong wind, has magnificently
cleared the air, freeing you from a fated lifetime
of brutal tyranny at the hands of sin and death. God
went for the jugular when he sent his
own Son. He didn't deal with the problem
as something remote and unimportant.
In his Son, Jesus, he personally took on the human
condition, entered the disordered mess
of struggling humanity in order to set it right once
and for all…. What the law code asked for but we
couldn't deliver is accomplished as we, instead of
redoubling our own efforts, simply embrace what
the Spirit is doing in us…. Those who trust God's
action in them find that God's Spirit is in them—
living and breathing God!

ROMANS 8:2-6 MSG

For it is God who works in you,
both to will and to work for his good pleasure.

PHILIPPIANS 2:13 ESV

*As we pray... God is inviting
us deeper in and higher up.
There is training in
righteousness,
transforming power, new joy,
deeper intimacy.*

RICHARD J. FOSTER

Contentment

I have learned to be content in whatever circumstances I am. I know how to get along with humble means, and I also know how to live in prosperity; in any and every circumstance I have learned the secret of being filled and going hungry, both of having abundance and suffering need. I can do all things through Him who strengthens me.

PHILIPPIANS 4:11-13 NASB

Godliness with contentment is great gain.
For we brought nothing into the world,
and we can take nothing out of it.
But if we have food and clothing,
we will be content with that.

1 TIMOTHY 6:6-8 NIV

When my anxious thoughts multiply within me,
Your consolations delight my soul.

PSALM 94:19 NASB

Where you are right now is God's place for you.
Live and obey and love and believe right there.

1 CORINTHIANS 7:17 MSG

*Contentment is not the fulfillment
of what you want; it is the realization
and appreciation of how much
you already have.*

Fulfilled Promises

Not one word of all the good words which the Lord
your God spoke concerning you has failed; all have
been fulfilled for you, not one of them has failed.

JOSHUA 23:14 NASB

Remember your promise to me;
it is my only hope.
Your promise revives me;
it comforts me in all my troubles....
Your eternal word, O Lord,
stands firm in heaven.
Your faithfulness extends to every generation,
as enduring as the earth you created.
Your regulations remain true to this day,
for everything serves your plans....
Your promises have been thoroughly tested;
that is why I love them so much.

PSALM 119:49-50, 89-91, 140 NLT

The fulfillment of God's promise depends entirely on trusting God and his way, and then simply embracing him and what he does.
God's promise arrives as pure gift.

ROMANS 4:16 MSG

GOD promises to love me all day, sing songs all through the night! My life is God's prayer.

PSALM 42:8 MSG

We may...depend upon God's promises, for...He will be as good as His word.

MATTHEW HENRY

Watching Over You

Whoever dwells in the shelter of the Most High
will rest in the shadow of the Almighty.
I will say of the LORD,
"He is my refuge and my fortress,
my God, in whom I trust."...
If you say, "The LORD is my refuge,"
and you make the Most High your dwelling,
no harm will overtake you,
no disaster will come near your tent.
For he will command his angels concerning you
to guard you in all your ways.

PSALM 91:1-2, 9-11 NIV

The LORD says, "I will guide you along
the best pathway for your life.
I will advise you and watch over you."

PSALM 32:8 NLT

But you, O LORD, are a shield around me;
you are my glory, the one who holds my head high.
I cried out to the LORD,
and he answered me from his holy mountain.
I lay down and slept,
yet I woke up in safety,
for the LORD was watching over me.

PSALM 3:3-5 NLT

God is constantly taking
knowledge of me in love
and watching over me for my good.

J. I. PACKER

Light in the Darkness

In the beginning was the Word, and the
Word was with God, and the Word was God.
He was in the beginning with God. All things came
into being through Him, and apart from Him nothing
came into being that has come into being. In Him was
life, and the life was the Light of men.

JOHN 1:1-4 NASB

For God, who said, "Let light shine out
of darkness," made his light shine in our hearts to
give us the light of the knowledge of God's glory
displayed in the face of Christ. But we have
this treasure in jars of clay to show that this
all-surpassing power is from God and not from us.

2 CORINTHIANS 4:6-7 NIV

Jesus spoke to them, saying,
"I am the light of the world.
Whoever follows me will not walk in darkness,
but will have the light of life."

JOHN 8:12 ESV

Open wide the windows of our spirits
and fill us full of light;
open wide the door of our hearts,
that we may receive and entertain
You with all our powers of adoration.

CHRISTINA ROSSETTI

I Will Seek Him

The LORD is my light and my salvation—
whom shall I fear?...
One thing I ask from the LORD,
this only do I seek:
that I may dwell in the house of the LORD
all the days of my life,
to gaze on the beauty of the LORD
and to seek him in his temple.
For in the day of trouble
he will keep me safe in his dwelling;
he will hide me in the shelter of his sacred tent
and set me high upon a rock....
Hear my voice when I call, LORD;
be merciful to me and answer me.
My heart says of you, "Seek his face!"
Your face, LORD, I will seek.

PSALM 27:1, 4-5, 7-8 NIV

I love those who love me;
and those who diligently seek me will find me.

PROVERBS 8:17 NASB

God is not an elusive dream
or a phantom to chase,
but a divine person to know.
He does not avoid us, but seeks
us. When we seek Him,
the contact is instantaneous.

NEVA COYLE

Bought with a Price

Don't be afraid, I've redeemed you. I've called
your name. You're mine. When you're in over your
head, I'll be there with you. When you're in rough
waters, you will not go down. When you're between
a rock and a hard place, it won't be a dead end—
Because I am God, your personal God,
The Holy of Israel, your Savior. I paid a huge
price for you...! *That's* how much you mean to me!
That's how much I love you!

ISAIAH 43:1-4 MSG

For you know that it was not with
perishable things such as silver or gold
that you were redeemed...but with the precious
blood of Christ, a lamb without blemish or defect.

1 PETER 1:18-19 NIV

Do you not know that your body is a temple
of the Holy Spirit within you, whom you
have from God? You are not your own,
for you were bought with a price.
So glorify God in your body.

1 CORINTHIANS 6:19–20 ESV

You are in the Beloved...
therefore infinitely dear to the Father,
unspeakably precious to Him.

NORMAN F. DOWTY

Lord of Lords

He raised Christ from the dead and seated
him at his right hand in the heavenly realms,
far above all rule and authority, power and
dominion, and every name that is invoked, not
only in the present age but also
in the one to come. And God placed all things
under his feet and appointed him
to be head over everything for the church,
which is his body, the fullness of him
who fills everything in every way.

EPHESIANS 1:20-23 NIV

For in Him all the fullness of Deity
dwells in bodily form, and in Him
you have been made complete.

COLOSSIANS 2:9-10 NASB

Our Lord Jesus Christ...who is the blessed and only
Sovereign, the King of kings and Lord of lords, who
alone has immortality, who dwells in unapproachable
light, whom no one has ever seen or can see. To him
be honor and eternal dominion. Amen.

1 TIMOTHY 6:14-16 ESV

*Jesus Christ...is not man
becoming God, but God
Incarnate, God coming into
human flesh, coming into it from
outside. His life is the Highest
and the Holiest entering in
at the lowliest door.*

OSWALD CHAMBERS

You're Worth It

Now in Christ Jesus you who formerly were far off
have been brought near by the blood of Christ.
For He Himself is our peace.

EPHESIANS 2:13-14 NASB

Christ arrives right on time to make this happen. He
didn't, and doesn't, wait for us to get ready.
He presented himself for this sacrificial
death when we were far too weak and rebellious
to do anything to get ourselves ready....
We can understand someone dying for a person worth
dying for.... But God put his love on the line for us by
offering his Son in sacrificial death
while we were of no use whatever to him.

ROMANS 5:6-8 MSG

Are not five sparrows sold for two pennies?
Yet not one of them is forgotten by God.
Indeed, the very hairs of your head
are all numbered. Don't be afraid;
you are worth more than many sparrows.

LUKE 12:6-7 NIV

*The God who created, names,
and numbers the stars in the heavens
also numbers the hairs of my head....
What matters to me matters to Him,
and that changes my life.*

ELISABETH ELLIOT

That All May Know

Do not let this one fact escape your notice,
beloved, that with the Lord one day is like
a thousand years, and a thousand years
like one day. The Lord is not slow about
His promise, as some count slowness,
but is patient toward you, not wishing for any to
perish but for all to come to repentance.

2 PETER 3:8-9 NASB

My purpose is that they may be encouraged
in heart and united in love, so that they may
have the full riches of complete understanding,
in order that they may know the mystery of
God, namely, Christ, in whom are hidden all the
treasures of wisdom and knowledge.

COLOSSIANS 2:2-3 NIV

Go therefore and make disciples of all the nations,
baptizing them in the name of the Father and the Son
and the Holy Spirit, teaching them to observe all that
I commanded you; and lo, I am with you always,
even to the end of the age.

MATTHEW 28:19-20 NASB

*God has always used
ordinary people to carry out
His extraordinary mission.
Ordinary people filled with
His transforming life to be used
in extraordinary ways.
Ordinary people like you.*

The God We Serve

"The LORD is my portion," says my soul,
"therefore I will hope in him."
The LORD is good to those who wait for him,
to the soul who seeks him.

LAMENTATIONS 3:24-25 ESV

I waited patiently for the LORD to help me,
and he turned to me and heard my cry.
He lifted me out of the pit of despair,
out of the mud and the mire.
He set my feet on solid ground
and steadied me as I walked along.
He has given me a new song to sing,
a hymn of praise to our God.
Many will see what he has done and be amazed.
They will put their trust in the LORD.
Oh, the joys of those who trust the LORD.

PSALM 40:1-4 NLT

If you, Lord, kept a record of sins,
Lord, who could stand?
But with you there is forgiveness,
so that we can, with reverence, serve you.

PSALM 130:3-4 NIV

You, Lord, are a compassionate and gracious God,
slow to anger, abounding in love and faithfulness.

PSALM 86:15 NIV

The loving God we serve has immeasurable compassion and tenderness toward each of us throughout our lives.

DR. JAMES DOBSON

Sunrise to Sunset

The heavens are telling the glory of God;
and the firmament proclaims his handiwork.

PSALM 19:1 NRSV

If I rise on the wings of the dawn,
if I settle on the far side of the sea,
even there your hand will guide me,
your right hand will hold me fast.

PSALM 139:9-10 NIV

God is sheer mercy and grace;
not easily angered, he's rich in love....
As far as sunrise is from sunset,
he has separated us from our sins.

PSALM 103:8, 12 MSG

Let me hear Your lovingkindness in the morning;
For I trust in you.

PSALM 143:8 NASB

Where morning dawns, where evening fades,
you call forth songs of joy.

PSALM 65:8 NIV

The day is done, the sun has set,
Yet light still tints the sky;
My heart stands still in reverence,
For God is passing by.

RUTH ALLA WAGER

My Personal Guide

I'll take the hand of those who don't know
the way, who can't see where they're going.
I'll be a personal guide to them, directing them
through unknown country. I'll be right there
to show them what roads to take, make sure they
don't fall into the ditch. These are the things
I'll be doing for them—sticking with them,
not leaving them for a minute.

ISAIAH 42:16 MSG

Show me your ways, Lord,
teach me your paths.
Guide me in your truth and teach me,
for you are God my Savior,
and my hope is in you all day long.

PSALM 25:4-5 NIV

Whether you turn to the right or to the left,
your ears will hear a voice behind you, saying,
"This is the way; walk in it."

ISAIAH 30:21 NIV

The Lord is good and does what is right;
he shows the proper path to those who go astray.
He leads the humble in doing right,
teaching them his way.

PSALM 25:8-9 NLT

*We have ample evidence that
the Lord is able to guide. The
promises cover every imaginable
situation. All we need to do is to
take the hand He stretches out.*

ELISABETH ELLIOT

I Will Give You Rest

The promise of "arrival" and "rest" is still there for
God's people. God himself is at rest. And at the end
of the journey we'll surely rest with God. So let's
keep at it and eventually arrive at the place of rest.

HEBREWS 4:9-11 MSG

Yes, my soul, find rest in God;
my hope comes from him.

PSALM 62:5 NIV

Come to me, all you who labor and are heavy laden,
and I will give you rest. Take My yoke upon you and
learn from Me, for I am gentle and lowly
in heart, and you will find rest for your souls.
For My yoke is easy, and My burden is light.

MATTHEW 11:28-30 NKJV

I will refresh the weary and satisfy the faint.

JEREMIAH 31:25 NIV

Then Jesus said, "Let's go off by ourselves
to a quiet place and rest awhile."

MARK 6:31 NLT

*Our ever growing soul
and its capacities can be satisfied only
in the infinite God. As water is restless
until it reaches its level, so the soul
has no peace until it rests in God.*

SADHU SUNDAR SINGH

Prepared Beforehand

God, being rich in mercy, because of His
great love with which He loved us...raised us
up with Him, and seated us with Him in the heavenly
places in Christ Jesus, so that in
the ages to come He might show the
surpassing riches of His grace in
kindness toward us in Christ Jesus.

For by grace you have been saved through faith; and
that not of yourselves, it is the gift of God; not as a
result of works, so that no one may boast.

For we are His workmanship, created in Christ Jesus
for good works, which God prepared beforehand so
that we would walk in them.

EPHESIANS 2:4, 6-10 NASB

"What no eye has seen, what no ear has heard, and what no human mind has conceived"—the things God has prepared for those who love him.

1 CORINTHIANS 2:9 NIV

God is preparing me for good works and preparing good works for me to do. How can I allow Him to change me into who He created me to be so I can do the work He created me to do?

In Him

The God who made the world and everything
in it is the Lord of heaven and earth and does not
live in temples built by human hands. And he is not
served by human hands, as if he needed anything.
Rather, he himself gives everyone life and breath and
everything else.... God did this so that they would
seek him and perhaps reach out for him and find him,
though he is not far from any one of us.
"For in him we live and move and have our being."

ACTS 17:24-25, 27-28 NIV

For from Him and through Him and to Him
are all things. To Him be the glory forever. Amen.

ROMANS 11:36 NASB

The LORD is gracious and merciful,
slow to anger and abounding in steadfast love.
The LORD is good to all, and his compassion is over
all that he has made.... The LORD is faithful
in all his words, and gracious in all his deeds.

PSALM 145:8-9, 13 NRSV

Recognizing who we are in
Christ and aligning our life
with God's purpose for us gives a
sense of destiny.... It gives form
and direction to our life.

JEAN FLEMING

Talking to God

When you pray, go away by yourself,
shut the door behind you, and pray to your
Father in private. Then your Father,
who sees everything, will reward you.
When you pray, don't babble on and on...
for your Father knows exactly
what you need even before you ask him!

MATTHEW 6:6-8 NLT

Embrace this God-life. Really embrace it, and
nothing will be too much for you.... That's why
I urge you to pray for absolutely everything,
ranging from small to large. Include everything
as you embrace this
God-life, and you'll get God's everything.

MARK 11:22-24 MSG

We do not know what we ought to pray for, but the
Spirit himself intercedes for us through wordless
groans. And he who searches our hearts knows the
mind of the Spirit, because the Spirit intercedes for
God's people in accordance with the will of God.

ROMANS 8:26-27 NIV

Pray to the Father. He loves to help.

JAMES 1:5 MSG

When life tumbles in and
problems overwhelm us...
how reassuring it is to know that
the Spirit makes intercession for us!

HAZEL C. LEE

His Thoughts

Your thoughts—how rare, how beautiful!
God, I'll never comprehend them!
I couldn't even begin to count them—
any more than I could count the sand of the sea.
Oh, let me rise in the morning
and live always with you!

PSALM 139:17-18 MSG

How great are your works, Lᴏʀᴅ,
how profound your thoughts!

PSALM 92:5 NIV

Take a long, hard look. See how great he is—infinite,
greater than anything you could ever imagine or
figure out!

JOB 36:26 MSG

Many, O Lᴏʀᴅ my God,
are the wonders which You have done,
And Your thoughts toward us;
There is none to compare with You.
If I would declare and speak of them,
They would be too numerous to count.

PSALM 40:5 NASB

God, the master artist, is most
concerned about expressing
Himself—His thoughts and
His intentions—through what
He paints in our character....
He wants to paint a beautiful
portrait of His Son
in and through your life.

JONI EARECKSON TADA

Our Help and Shield

I will lift up my eyes to the hills—
From whence comes my help?
My help comes from the LORD,
Who made heaven and earth.
He will not allow your foot to be moved;
He who keeps you will not slumber.
Behold, He who keeps Israel
Shall neither slumber nor sleep.
The LORD is your keeper;
The LORD is your shade at your right hand.
The sun shall not strike you by day,
Nor the moon by night.
The LORD shall preserve you from all evil;
He shall preserve your soul.
The LORD shall preserve your going out
and your coming in
from this time forth, and even forevermore.

PSALM 121:1-8 NKJV

Our soul waits for the Lᴏʀᴅ;
he is our help and our shield.
For our heart is glad in him,
because we trust in his holy name.
Let your steadfast love, O Lᴏʀᴅ, be upon us,
even as we hope in you.

PSALM 33:20-22 ESV

We have a Father in heaven who is
almighty, who loves His children
as He loves His only-begotten Son,
and whose very joy and delight
it is to...help them at all times
and under all circumstances.

GEORGE MUELLER

All Things Work Together

We look at this Son and see God's
original purpose in everything created.
For everything, absolutely everything,
above and below, visible and invisible,
rank after rank after rank of angels—everything
got started in him and finds
its purpose in him. He was there before any
of it came into existence and holds it
all together right up to this moment....
So spacious is he, so roomy, that everything
of God finds its proper place in him
without crowding. Not only that, but all the
broken and dislocated pieces of the universe—
people and things, animals and atoms—
get properly fixed and fit together
in vibrant harmonies.

COLOSSIANS 1:16-17, 19-20 MSG

We know that all things work together
for good to them that love God, to them who
are the called according to his purpose.

ROMANS 8:28 KJV

May God himself, the God who makes everything holy and
whole, make you holy and whole.

1 THESSALONIANS 5:23 MSG

*Taken separately, the experiences of
life can work harm and not good.
Taken together, they make a pattern
of blessing and strength the like
of which the world does not know.*

V. RAYMOND EDMAN

Created for His Pleasure

So God created human beings in his own image.
In the image of God he created them;
male and female he created them.

GENESIS 1:27 NLT

For you created my inmost being;
you knit me together in my mother's womb.
I praise you because I am fearfully
and wonderfully made;
your works are wonderful, I know that full well.

PSALM 139:13-14 NIV

Thou art worthy, O Lord, to receive glory and honour
and power: for thou hast created all things, and for
thy pleasure they are and were created.

REVELATION 4:11 KJV

LORD, you are our Father.
We are the clay, and you are the potter.
We are all formed by your hand.

ISAIAH 64:8 NLT

Create in me a clean heart, O God;
and renew a right spirit within me.

PSALM 51:10 KJV

*In the very beginning it was God who...
made us in His own image. God was
spirit and He gave us a spirit so that
He could come into us and mingle His
own life with our life.*

JEANNE GUYON

Faithfulness Extended

Therefore, brothers and sisters, since we have
confidence to enter the Most Holy Place by the blood
of Jesus, by a new and living way opened
for us through the curtain, that is, his body,
and since we have a great priest over the house
of God, let us draw near to God with a sincere
heart and with the full assurance that faith brings,
having our hearts sprinkled to cleanse us from a
guilty conscience and having our bodies washed with
pure water. Let us hold unswervingly to the hope we
profess, for he who promised is faithful.

HEBREWS 10:19-23 NIV

May God the Father and the Lord Jesus Christ give
you love with faithfulness. May God's grace be
eternally upon all who love our Lord Jesus Christ.

EPHESIANS 6:23-24 NLT

For great is your love, reaching to the heavens;
your faithfulness reaches to the skies.
Be exalted, O God, above the heavens;
let your glory be over all the earth.

PSALM 57:10-11 NIV

*Swim through your temptations
and troubles.... Run to the promises:
they [are] our Lord's branches
hanging over the water, that [His]
children may take a grip of them.*

SAMUEL RUTHERFORD

Safe Haven

He rescues you from hidden traps,
shields you from deadly hazards.
His huge outstretched arms protect you—
under them you're perfectly safe;
his arms fend off all harm....
"If you'll hold on to me for dear life," says GOD,
"I'll get you out of any trouble.
I'll give you the best of care
if you'll only get to know and trust me.
Call me and I'll answer, be at your side in bad times;
I'll rescue you, then throw you a party.
I'll give you...a long drink of salvation!"

PSALM 91:3-6, 14-15 MSG

You are God, my only safe haven.

PSALM 43:2 NLT

They cried out to the LORD in their trouble,
And he brought them out of their distress.
He stilled the storm to a whisper;
the waves of the sea were hushed.
They were glad when it grew calm,
and he guided them to their desired haven.

PSALM 107:28-30 NIV

Calm me, O Lord, as you stilled the storm,
Still me, O Lord, keep me from harm.
Let all the tumult within me cease,
Enfold me, Lord, in your peace.

CELTIC TRADITIONAL

The Apple of His Eye

Who shall separate us from the love of Christ?
Shall trouble or hardship or persecution
or famine or nakedness or danger or sword?...
No, in all these things we are more than conquerors
through him who loved us. For I am convinced that
neither death nor life, neither angels nor demons,
neither the present nor the future, nor any powers,
neither height nor depth, nor anything else in all
creation, will be able to separate us from the love of
God that is in Christ Jesus our Lord.

ROMANS 8:35, 37-39 NIV

Show me the wonders of your great love....
Keep me as the apple of your eye;
hide me in the shadow of your wings.

PSALM 17:7-8 NIV

The LORD will work out his plans for my life—
for your faithful love, O LORD, endures forever.

PSALM 138:8 NLT

*Let your faith in Christ,
the omnipresent One,
be in the quiet confidence
that He will every day
and every moment keep you
as the apple of His eye,
keep you in perfect peace.*

ANDREW MURRAY

Glorious Living

Because of the sacrifice of the Messiah...we're a
free people—free of penalties and punishments
chalked up by all our misdeeds. And not just
barely free, either. Abundantly free!

He thought of everything, provided for
everything we could possibly need, letting us in
on the plans he took such delight in making. He
set it all out before us in Christ,
a long range plan in which everything would
be brought together and summed up in him....

It's in Christ that we find out who we are
and what we are living for. Long before we first
heard of Christ and got our hopes up, he had his
eye on us, had designs on us for glorious living,
part of the overall purpose he is working out in
everything and everyone.

EPHESIANS 1:7-9, 11-12 MSG

May the favor of the Lord our God rest upon us;
establish the work of our hands for us—
yes, establish the work of our hands.

PSALM 90:17 NIV

How blessed is everyone who fears the LORD,
Who walks in His ways.

PSALM 128:1 NASB

The patterns of our days are always rearranging, but God's purpose remains the same. His design is for glorious living, graced with His love and favor.

Trust Steadily

Truly my soul finds rest in God;

my salvation comes from him.

Truly he is my rock and my salvation;

he is my fortress, I will never be shaken....

My salvation and my honor depend on God;

he is my mighty rock, my refuge.

Trust in him at all times, you people;

pour out your hearts to him,

for God is our refuge....

One thing God has spoken,

two things have I heard:

"Power belongs to you, God,

and with you, Lord, is unfailing love."

PSALM 62:1-2,7-8,11-12 NIV

Rest in the LORD, and wait patiently for him.

PSALM 37:7 KJV

Trust in the LORD with all your heart,
And lean not on your own understanding;
In all your ways acknowledge Him,
And He shall direct your paths.

PROVERBS 3:5-6 NKJV

*Infinite and yet personal, personal and
yet infinite, God may be trusted
because He is the True One.
He is true, He acts truly,
and He speaks truly....
Truthfulness is therefore foundational
for His trustworthiness.*

OS GUINNESS

Steadfast Love

The steadfast love of the LORD never ceases, his
mercies never come to an end; they are new every
morning; great is your faithfulness.

LAMENTATIONS 3:22-23 NRSV

Enter into His gates with thanksgiving,
And into His courts with praise.
Be thankful to Him, and bless His name.
For the LORD is good;
His mercy is everlasting,
And His truth endures to all generations.

PSALM 100:4-5 NKJV

All the paths of the LORD are
steadfast love and faithfulness,
for those who keep his covenant and his testimonies.

PSALM 25:10 ESV

Give thanks to the Lord, for he is good,
for his steadfast love endures forever.
Give thanks to the God of gods,
for his steadfast love endures forever.
Give thanks to the Lord of lords,
for his steadfast love endures forever;
to him who alone does great wonders,
for his steadfast love endures forever.

PSALM 136:1-4 ESV

Whether we feel strong or weak in our faith, we remember that our assurance is...in the faithfulness of God. We focus on His trustworthiness and especially on His steadfast love.

RICHARD J. FOSTER

I Will Praise Him

I will bless the LORD at all times:
his praise shall continually be in my mouth.

PSALM 34:1 KJV

Praise the LORD!
Praise God in His sanctuary;
Praise Him in His mighty firmament!
Praise Him for His mighty acts;
Praise Him according to His excellent greatness!
Praise Him with the sound of the trumpet;
Praise Him with the lute and harp!
Praise Him with the timbrel and dance;
Praise Him with stringed instruments and flutes!
Praise Him with loud cymbals;
Praise Him with clashing cymbals!
Let everything that has breath praise the LORD.
Praise the LORD!

PSALM 150:1-6 NKJV

I will give thanks to the LORD with all my heart;
I will tell of all Your wonders.
I will be glad and exult in You;
I will sing praise to Your name, O Most High.

PSALM 9:1-2 NASB

*Dear Lord,
grant me the grace of wonder.
Surprise me, amaze me, awe me
in every crevice of Your universe....
Each day enrapture me with
Your marvelous things without number.*

ABRAHAM JOSHUA HESCHEL

Everything You Need

Don't fuss about what's on the table at mealtimes
or if the clothes in your closet are in fashion.
There is far more to your inner life than the food
you put in your stomach, more to your outer
appearance than the clothes you hang on your body.
Look at the ravens, free and unfettered,
not tied down to a job description,
carefree in the care of God. And you count far more.

LUKE 12:22-24 MSG

His divine power has given us everything
we need for a godly life through our knowledge
of him who called us by his own glory
and goodness. Through these he has given
us his very great and precious promises.

2 PETER 1:3-4 NIV

God will generously provide all you need.
Then you will always have everything you need
and plenty left over to share with others.

2 CORINTHIANS 9:8 NLT

I am like a luxuriant fruit tree.
Everything you need is to be found in me.

HOSEA 14:8 MSG

Where there is faith, there is love.
Where there is love, there is peace.
Where there is peace, there is God.
Where there is God, there is no need.

A Fine Vineyard

At that same time, a fine vineyard will appear.

There's something to sing about!

I, God, tend it.

I keep it well-watered.

I keep careful watch over it

so that no one can damage it....

Even if it gives me thistles and thornbushes,

I'll just pull them out

and burn them up.

Let that vine cling to me for safety,

let it find a good and whole life with me,

let it hold on for a good and whole life.

ISAIAH 27:2-5 MSG

The river of God has plenty of water;

it provides a bountiful harvest.

PSALM 65:9 NLT

Abide in Me, and I in you. As the branch cannot
bear fruit of itself unless it abides in the vine,
so neither can you unless you abide in Me.
I am the vine, you are the branches; he who abides
in Me and I in him, he bears much fruit,
for apart from Me you can do nothing.

JOHN 15:4-5 NASB

It is God's knowledge of me,
His careful husbanding
of the ground of my being,
His constant presence in the garden
of my little life that guarantees my joy.

W. PHILLIP KELLER

Ever the Same

Of old you laid the foundation of the earth,

and the heavens are the work of your hands.

They will perish, but you will remain;

they will all wear out like a garment.

You will change them like a robe,

and they will pass away,

but you are the same, and your years have no end.

PSALM 102:25-27 ESV

Oh, blessed be God!

He didn't go off and leave us.

He didn't abandon us defenseless....

God's strong name is our help,

the same God who made heaven and earth.

PSALM 124:6, 8 MSG

The Lord merely spoke,
and the heavens were created....
Let the whole world fear the Lord,
and let everyone stand in awe of him.
For when he spoke, the world began!

PSALM 33:6-9 NLT

Although I may experience many ups
and downs in my emotions and often
feel great shifts in my inner life,
you remain the same.... O Lord,
sea of love and goodness...let me know
that there is ebb and flow...
but that the sea remains the sea.

HENRI J. M. NOUWEN

He Is Life Itself

GOD, your God, will cut away the thick calluses
on your heart and your children's hearts, freeing
you to love GOD, your God,
with your whole heart and soul and live,
really live.... And you will make a new start,
listening obediently to GOD, keeping all his
commandments that I'm commanding you today.
GOD, your God, will outdo himself
in making things go well for you....
Love GOD, your God. Walk in his ways.
Keep his commandments, regulations,
and rules so that you will live, really live,
live exuberantly, blessed by GOD....
Love GOD, your God, listening obediently
to him, firmly embracing him.
Oh yes, he is life itself.

DEUTERONOMY 30:6, 8-9, 16, 20 MSG

118

I have come that they may have life,
and have it to the full.... I am the good shepherd;
I know my sheep and my sheep know me—
just as the Father knows me and I know
the Father—and I lay down my life for the sheep.

JOHN 10:10, 14-15 NIV

*Life itself, every bit of health
that we enjoy, every hour of liberty
and free enjoyment...
comes from the hand of God.*

BILLY GRAHAM

An Invitation

If you have ever:
    questioned if this is all there is to life...
    wondered what happens when you die...
    felt a longing for purpose or significance...
    wrestled with resurfacing anger...
    struggled to forgive someone...
    known there is a "higher power" but couldn't define it...
    sensed you have a role to play in the world...
    experienced success and still felt empty afterward...
then consider Jesus.

A great teacher from two millennia ago, Jesus of Nazareth, the Son of God, freely chose to show our Maker's everlasting love for us by offering to take all of our flaws, darkness, death, and mistakes into His very body (1 Peter 2:24). The result was His death on a cross. But the story doesn't end there. God raised Him from the dead and invites us to believe this truth in our hearts and follow Jesus into eternal life.

If you confess with your mouth that Jesus is Lord and believe in your heart that God raised him from the dead, you will be saved. –ROMANS 10:9 NLT